A Mandatory Protection
Spiritual Fitness Bible Study for Daily Living

Honoré Nicole

Cadmus Publishing
www.cadmuspublishing.com

Copyright © 2022 Honoré Nicole

Cover Design: Cammry Lapka – Cammrylapkaart.com Cammrylapka@gmail.com

Published by Cadmus Publishing
www.cadmuspublishing.com
Haledon, NJ

Hardcover ISBN: 978-1-63751-480-1
Library of Congress Control Number: 2022919462

Unless otherwise noted, Scripture quotations are taken from the Holman Christian Standard Bible and the New Living Translation Study Bible.

All rights reserved. Copyright under Berne Copyright Convention, Universal Copyright Convention, and Pan-American Copyright Convention. No part of this book may be repro-duced, stored in a retrieval system, or transmitted in any form, or by any means, electronic, mechanical, photocopying, recording or otherwise, without prior permission of the author.

Table of Contents

Introduction 1
Preface 4
Study 1: The Gravity Of Our Words 15
Study 2: Super Excited 25
Study 3: His Priority 33
Study 4: Your Want to Matters 43
Study 5: The Highest Level 51
Study 6: Defining Moment 61
Study 7: Tested and Tried 71
Study 8: The Essence Of Who God IS 79
Study 9: Increase Your Praise 89
Study 10: Dismantle Your Idols 101
Study 11: The Greatest Treasure 113
Study 12: Most Qualified Defender 121
Acknowledgements of Praise 131

An Exclusive Revelation from Honore' Nicole to Her Friends

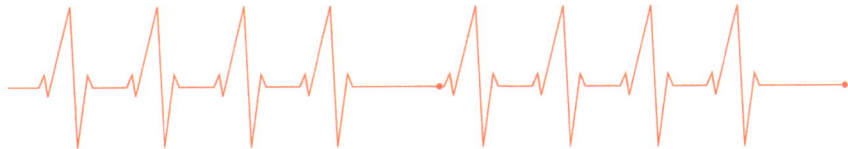

Dear Friends,

For over three and a half decades, the protection of God has been sustaining me, maintaining me, and shielding me. I disregarded and insulted His divine protection on my life for over ten years. However, about a decade ago, the protection of God was revealed to me through the most devastating loss I've experienced in my life so far. Surrounded by fear, interrogation, sweat, heartache, and pain in my worst hours, I was arrested and convicted of murder of the second degree within a year. I shared this chapter of my story, because I wanted and needed for all of you to hear it straight from me first. I'm not proud of some aspects of my past, but through the grace of God's protection, my past is exactly what God said it is "redeemed," because He is doing a new thing within me. I'm extremely grateful that my past does not define me. My past has purposefully changed me, causing and shaping me to travel down the path God had already laid out as my destiny.

If you can look far beyond the tragedy connected to my past and accept and receive the simplicity of this study by applying these biblical and spiritual principles aquired to your everyday life. Then you will understand, recognize, and agree that the greatest protection you will ever obtain is inclusive—and exclusively for you.

This is a message for all the beautiful, smart, glorious people of the world: you have to MAKE A PERSONAL DECISION: First, that God's supernatural protection is richly covering you and was granted to you through the blood shed by Jesus Christ—way before you were ever a You. Second, acknowledge the Holy Spirit as your protector who lives deep within you: leading, guiding, and correcting you. Third, by faith, you have to accept the truth that His protection is immeasurable because it goes far beyond your past, present, and future.

Remember This:

God's divine protection will not just stabilize your life, but also stabilize the lives of others as well. His protection is mandatory, full of power, and will never change, not even in your worst hours. The protection of God is supernatural, overflowing with grace, power, and authority. His divine covering is multi-generational, you won't just strive, but He promised that you will thrive!

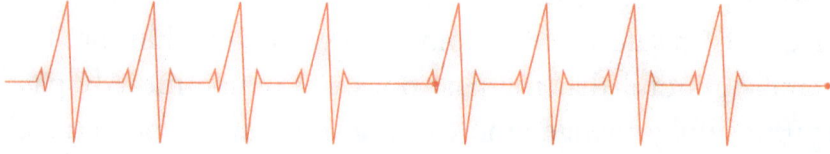

His protection did it for **Me**...

...and it will do it for **You**.

Introduction

"First and foremost, in our natural, human state, we did not choose divine protection. Whereas, supernaturally, through God's point of view, divine protection chose us before the creation of the earth."
~Honoré Nicole

INTRODUCTION

Moment by moment, God is constantly teaching me to holistically trust His divine protection in every area of my life. Often, the Lord challenges me to dismantle my humanly-average idea of what His supernatural protection should look like, feel like, or be like in my life. He is stretching me to continuously look beyond the familiar and walk into the unfamiliar the path and bridge to my hidden destiny. Only by the grace and power of the Holy Spirit do I believe I am able to achieve the unachievable, reach the unreachable, and heal the incurable (wounded hearts). I'm grateful for the presence of God's protection in my life, because He knew I could have never completed this Bible study on my own strength. By faith, He sealed me with His strength, His blessing, His wisdom, and His anointing, enabling me with the spirit of excellence to complete my part because the Most High God is faithful, and He has already completed His part.

Pivotal moment: for the last two and a half years, God has been effectively penetrating and filling my mind, heart, thoughts, and spirit, urging me to pay close attention to how His revolutionary protection is shielding the aura world around me. After taking notice and accepting the truth of His protection, God uncovered and revealed how I could take His divine protection and make it: universal, fundamental, relevant, and purposeful in my life first, in the lives of others, and in the lives of our future generations. God's divine protection is E-V-E-R-Y-T-H-I-N-G, and I am certain that He has already provided me with everything I need. Because the Holy Spirit is in alignment, orchestrating every significant detail appointed to my super(natural) existence. I understand God's supernatural protection is not just covering and providing for me, but also covering and providing for others who were created uniquely different than me.

Although I have my daily struggles, I was created on purpose, I am here today with purpose, and I am serving the people of this world because it is God's purpose. In fact, it is not God's purpose for the darkness of this world to be closing in all round me, but I vowed not to allow the fear of darkness to get inside of me. Instead of focusing on the darkness, I am escaping and overcoming the darkness by focusing and trusting the light of God's precious promises. I find inspiration and hope in being in close communion with the world's ultimate Protector, so in every way, each day, I am intentionally staying in forward motion.

Having a forward motion perspective means I am looking in front of me, not behind me. I am surrendering my defeated mentality for Christ's winning mentality, which enables me to stand sure— in the midst of turbulence, to stand sure ——in

the face of affliction and insecurity... overall, I am standing sure— with the foreknowledge of knowing that I might be inevitably opening myself up for the world to insult me, judge me, misinterpret my words, slander me because the surreal me is misunderstood, unless the world does the total opposite, and positively embrace me. Either way, deep within my soul, God empowered me with spiritual muscles and strategies to keep going. Go-Go-Go-Go: is all I hear! The famous words of my eldest brother, Derrick, who I hold dear. To my delight, I am humbly going: physically, mentally, emotionally, but most importantly spiritually. So, with all of this wisdom in mind, I am determined to be obedient by displaying how His protection is assured and how I can help others realize and understand how He can remove them from the pain of their dark prisonhoods by inserting them into the peace, protection, and care of God's royal priesthood. Therefore, in this moment, the grace of God has prepared and nourished me to embrace the challenge of knowing the Most Holy God can and will use my story to increase the amount of people who will see and enter into rest in His eternal Majesty!

Know This:

It's true, I was sentenced to a MANDATORY life sentence. But, I am certain that I was truly given a MANDATORY PROTECTION, as my divine covering, because the only person who can give and take away life, is God. In reality, God ushered me out of the pain and bitterness of my prisonhood only to bring me into the goodness and richness of HIS ROYAL PRIESTHOOD.

PREFACE

Imagine yourself standing in a cold court room at the age of 26, and the life you once knew is now obsolete. With no strength to be tough because you feel like a creampuff knowing that your former life, once filled with sounds of children playing, toy trucks, video games, smiles, and laughter, combined with beautiful ironic noises coming out of the mouths of two tiny little people, ages 2 and 5.

Now, reimagine yourself standing in this same cold court room, hearing the sound of a gavel (bang) after just being sentence by a female court judge to a mandatory life sentence at hard labor without the benefit of parole, probation, or suspension of sentence, because a month and a half ago, you were just found guilty by an 10-2 non- unanimous jury. The ten guilty votes from ten of the jurors—means you have to spend the rest of your life in prison, and that is the end of your story. Can you imagine the pain and headache?

A MANDATORY PROTECTION

The excruciating pain of knowing that you just let those two tiny little people down, who routinely ran around the house yelling and screaming "mommaaaa" for everything, because in their tiny little brains they view you as their— "everything." Aftering hearing the sound of the gavel (bang) all the memories of those tiny little smiles immediately turn into heartbreaking frowns. (tears)

Truly, there are no words that can ever explain the pain in your soulbecause you were forced to exchange motherhood for prisonhood. Now, can you imagine the core of my mental, emotional, and spiritual pain?

Often, I have witnessed people say, "there are different levels of pain." But over the years, God has revealed to me that "pain is just pain". In fact, everyone has experienced some substance of pain, and if you have not, then at some point of your life, you will come across your own share of pain.

For instance, my literal pain is not your pain. But generally speaking, pain is just pain. My soul was overflowing with pain, hurt,shame, anxiety, and embarrassment, because I was forced to exchange motherhood for prisonhood, so once again, can you imagine my pain?

Now, lets take a step back—away from my pain, and lets take a step forward— towards your pain, because at the end of each day, remember pain is just pain. It's easy for others to notice my pain, which is attach to my prisonhood. My pain is visible, physical, literal, and it was an unwanted, unintentional devastating heart wrenching tragedy, which made "Breaking News," displaying proof of my unforgettable pain.(my soul cries out)

Literally, you may not be in physical chains, but your pain and your chains may be connected to you through both in-

ternal and external things. Primarily, your pain keeps you associated with your prison, which subjects you to stay in your chains. Theenemies of your pain can be a mixture of the following things: your relationships, your attitude, your mental state, your character, your perspective, your emotional state, your overindulgence, your pride, your medical condition, your overspending, your need for validation and acceptance, your spiritual state, all colliding together— pointing to more deeper things.

In essence, we are all human beings with human frailties: real feelings, real issues, and real pain, because we all are living in a unsafe forever changing —dark and painful "real world." So, regardless of your source of pain, fear, hurt, or the facades you are hiding behind, my goal is to help you identify, build, and navigate your way through your original rooted pain. By sharing the grace and power of God's supernatural-extraordinary protection, which will definitely change the pain game.

Despite my inflammatory severe pain, over the years, God has built and revealed within me the necessary need for me to recognize and acknowledge the presence of His divine protection. The Lord's protection is full of anointing, healing, power, and authority. In fact, the Spirit of God twisted and elevated my story.My prisonhood motivated me to elevated my personal belief, so I could realize that I was predestined to be apart of God's priesthood. By grace, my story can encourage more and more people to live under the Most High Protection, so one day they can see His unseen eternal glory.

Value This Twisted Elevation:

This spiritual fitness Bible study is for you because we all fit right in. Mysteriously, God's protection has a way of transforming our prisonhood into His hood, called PRIESTHOOD. So, in every way, each day, we have to deliberately minimize our prisonhood by maximizing God's mandatory protection which can only be found in His everlasting priesthood.

Understand This:

I do not profess to have all the answers concerning God's mandatory protection, but life has given me divine wisdom which I humbly share with you today, tomorrow, and for the rest of my days.

The Vision for This Bible Study:

My vision for this study is to create quality principals and illustrations utilizing biblical Scriptures to help others access the wisdom, richness, righteousness, and knowledge connected to the inheritance of God's overflowing goodness and protectiveness. However, many people fail to understand and recognize that God's protection is— life-sustaining and life-changing. Like most things in life, were learning how to condition and train our minds, hearts, and spirits to consciously "seek for" and "yearn after" heavenly protection on every level.

In essence, within these study lessons, we will practice imitating Jesus Christ's ways, standards, and life as our own ways, standards, and life. After repeatedly practicing and meditating on God's character and nature, we will eventually realize that

God's goodness and protectiveness is not performance based or contingent on our good or bad behaviors it is solely on the basis of learning and understanding that everything we need is already linked and established in the heavenly realms due to the "shed blood," "death," "burial," and "resurrection" of our Lord and Savior, Jesus Christ. In every respect, Christ's obedience permitted humanity (you and me) with the grace, power, and authority to believe, receive, and experience supernatural goodness and protection as God's ultimate gift that's available and universal for everyone. Remember: The Holy Spirit is your internal guide. Yet, it is your personal responsibility for you to foster and increase your focus by building, learning, and valuing the ways, standards, and life of Jesus Christ as your foundation for life.

How To Use This Spiritual Fitness Bible Study:

* As a 12 Day Challenge, a 12 Week Study, or Monthly (Month to Month) Study

* This is a comprehensive study where several different spiritual fitness tools are highlighted to specifically help you understand and deepen your wisdom and knowledge concerning kingdom protection. This study will help you grasp insightful truth connected to ancient biblical history. Then, you will learn how to practice and appreciate ancient wisdom. Applying these fundamental truths from biblical history to modern day society and real-life circumstances will help you and others learn from and live a life with divine purpose and passion.

* Within this study, there are 12 biblical Scriptures (emphasis on divine protection), 12 real life illustrations, 12 prayers of declaration (these prayers are meant to be spoken aloud because your words have the power of shaping and shifting your perspective and can help you release and remove the friction in the atmosphere), 12 in-depth practical applications, and 12 reflective notes (this is a personal writing area to help you express, amplify, and release your true feelings in a healthydirection upwardly).

Why Is It Essential for You To Utilize This Study:

* To discover how God's incredible protection is for you. Also, you can help others comprehend how to recognize supernatural protection in their lives.

* This study teaches you how to focus on your specific target. Such as: learning how to deal with different stigmas and fears, discovering how to experience supernatural protection even under the world's phenomenon of feeling unprotected, and/or learning how to cope with other particular stressful dilemmas that emerge daily in this complex surreal world we live in.

* This spiritual fitness can challenge, train, and equip you to disconnect from the anxiety of this world by learning how to gradually trust and depend on God as your ultimate source for spiritual awareness, purpose, physical strength, passion, and protection.

* Highlighting the importance on why it's fundamental for everyone to have an upward perspective because God's unidentifiable protection is not easy to grasp because it's supernatural, impactful, and transformational. The result of embracing and executing this truth will affect your daily thoughts, practices, and actions positively.

* Within this study, there are insightful wisdoms to remind and show you how to rest in God's peace, protection, and contentment, rather than worrying about situations that only the Lord can change.

* You will also learn to build and maintain an in-depth relationship with God the Father, Son, and Holy Spirit.

You choose how you want to use AMP Spiritual Fitness for Daily Living:

You have options.

Mark your option below.

- ☐ A 12 Day Challenge
- ☐ A 12 Week Study
- ☐ A 12 Monthly Study (month-to-month)

Study 1

"Our thoughts become our words. Therefore, it is vitally important that we choose life-generating thoughts. When we do, right words will follow."
~Joyce Meyer

THE GRAVITY OF OUR WORDS

"Lord, set up a guard for my mouth keep watch at the door on my lips." (Psalm 141: 3 HCSB)

Have you ever asked the Lord to protect the words that come out your mouth? Do you understand your spoken words are extremely impactful and powerful? In fact, the existence of the entire universe came into fruition by the seed of God's spoken words (Genesis 1). The greatest teacher said, "The seed is the Word." Christ spoke the Truth, which is the Word. Jesus' words openly displayed supernatural power and pledge allegiance to the fact and truth that 'words are powerful'! Words have the physical and emotional force of building up or tearing down.

In retrospect, I recognize my grandmother's words were exceptional and always emulated the abundant grace of God's words. Often she said, "Think about what you are going to say before you say it," and, "if you have nothing good to say, then don't say anything at all." Have you heard these sayings? Frankly, her wise words align with the psalmist's obvious advice to ask God to keep guardrails around your words. Let your words reflect Jesus' loving words which produce *healing, encouragement, edification, truthfulness, purity, correction, gentleness, humility, and patience.* **Read Colossians 3:12.**

Indeed, let's keep Jesus' loving words in mind, because in today's forever changing society, the words you speak are not just spoken words. Your words are also connected to texting, emailing, and posting on social media. The gravity of your words has extraordinary power! Let's not downplay the weight of your words, or ignore your words and actions, because they reflect what flows out of your hearts (Proverbs 27:19).This is especially true for a heart that refuses to surrender to Christ. Outside of Christ, your words are abusive and arrogant. They are actually enemies to your soul (mind, will, and emotion). Allow your words to build up rather than tear down. **Read Ephesians 4:29-32.**

If you want your words to increase your faith, and help positively transcend someone else's motivation, confidence, and strength then say out loud. *"Lord, may the words of my mouth and the meditation of my heart be acceptable to You, Lord, my rock and my Redeemer, in Jesus' name Amen."* Psalm 19:14

A More In-depth Application On The Gravity Of Our Words

* God is the Creator of all good things, including words. Humanity is gifted with rich words. God's words are for His children, His words do not fight against His children. The Lord promises and words are Yes and Amen (1 Corinthians 1:20).
* The Lord's words determine and direct our lives.
* God loves the human race so much that He gave us His spoken words. We must speak His words instead of our fleshly words. His words are pure and anointed with righteousness and inspiration (2 Timothy 3:16-17).
* All of God's words are true and they breathe hope, life, peace, and eternity with Him.
* Believers, it is imperative that we take our words very seriously, because the tongue has the power to produce life or death (Proverbs 18:21).

Remember:

The words of Jesus produce life and the words of world produce death. Below is a list highlighting Jesus' words which are polar opposite from the world's words:

Jesus' Words Verses The World's Words

Loving	Bitter and Hateful
Corrective	Without Insight
Heals	Kills and Destroys
Reveals Purpose	Purposeless
Purifies	Filthy and Sinful
Gracious	Boastful
Provide Direction	Leads Astray
Destroys Evil Bondages	Creates Bondage and Insecurities
Produces Fruit	Fruitless
Perfects	Prideful
Kind and Compassionate	Unkind and Insensitive
Promotes Forgiveness	Promotes Unforgiveness
Selfless	Selfish

* Jesus' actions and words are contagious. His words fell on fertile ground leaving humanity with the greatest seed ever, His spoken words. His words are filled with amazing grace, love, and foresight.

A MANDATORY PROTECTION

* Let the revelation of Jesus' words establish your words and ministry (your life). Therefore, I challenge you to evaluate the core of your old language and allow your new and improved language to be empowered by the Holy Spirit. **Read 1 Timothy 4: 11-15**

_____

Now, imagine your words having the same healing power and authority as God's words. What will you say to yourself, God, and others?

Write your response here:
_____
_____
_____
_____
_____
_____

Now pray and ask God to help you to grow spiritually so your words and actions work together in harmony for His glory. Afterwards, seek and create opportunities to encourage yourself and others through your words and deeds. Remember, you will have to give an account for every idle word you speak. (Matthew 12:36-37).

Be encouraged, this takes practice and everything is a process!

Reflective Notes

The Gravity of our Words

A MANDATORY PROTECTION

STUDY 2

"I'm real excited. I'm so blessed to have so much peace and joy inside. I just can't keep quiet about it."
~Brian Welch

Super Excited

"For you have died, and your life is hidden with the Messiah in God." (Colossians 3:3 HCSB)

Excited! Excited! Excited! Excited! Excitement is a joyous feeling that makes a person feel great on the inside! Excitement releases and increases positive energy in the brain cells, according to experts. Anything that's ruminating on the inside will come alive and become real on the outside.

Do you get super excited about special occasions? What about cheering on your favorite sports team? Do you feel joy in your heart when a baby is born? Are you overly excited when you finally enter into that relationship you always desired? Do you feel proud when you land the key to your success? Were you ecstatic when you heard that you may qualify for an unexpected desposit from the IRS? Do you get all warm on the inside when are able to spend quality time with family and friends?

Now, I am sure, at lease one of these areas bring you joy and happiness. However, the totality of your joy and happiness cannot be dependent on external pleasures. External things can add to your joy and excitement, but they cannot be the complete substance of your joy and excitement. The substance of your joy must come from the kingdom of God completely. Perfect joy will alter who or what you depend on for joy. By faith the Holy Spirit will help you receive and maintain everlasting blessing through the Messiah. Jesus the Christ was stripped of His perfect joy, He gave the children of God lives filled with ultimate joy and peace. His joy is comforting and transformational. Your journey in life will never be the same, you are forever changed (tears). So, get excited, not just excited, but super excited because you have a real reason to live, thrive, and come alive!

If you are ready to move past the temporary excitements of this world and receive and maintain your supernatural gift of excitement, then say out loud. *"Lord, I am super excited that I can totally live, thrive, and come alive because everything I need (on earth) is hidden and knitted in the Messiah (in heaven)."*

A More In-depth Application Of Kingdom Excitement

* True excitement comes in the form of godly wisdom, knowledge, and understanding. If you are separated from Christ, you will never fully experience lasting excitement.

* Obtaining true gratification requires separation. Separating from our achievements, purposes, works, and skills by exploring the Fruit of the Spirit. God's gave us the Fruit of the Spirit as our foundation to broaden our enjoyment and discipline.

* The fruits of the spirit are permanent attributes that express the qualities of God the Father, Son, and Holy. Christ exhibited great humility and holiness while He was here on earth. The primary goal in life is for believers to live by Jesus' examples.

* The practical knowledge regarding the fruit of the spirit requires followers to abide. Believers must abide in God for their deep sense of enjoyment. Abiding in God means we have to learn how to obey and accept His path for actual satisfaction and excitement. Our excitement should not be contingent on certain feelings, events, or experiences. True joy is permanent, and it is rooted and grounded in the hidden work of the Messiah (the Cross).

* Kingdom excitement takes intentionality. You have to be intentional about seeking, reaching and understanding the wisdom and knowledge of God in heaven.

* In essence, nothing is wrong with allowing earthly aspirations and objects to add to your excitement. However, do not allow these desires to take over your yearnings for authentic wisdom and excitement that abide in heaven and is extended to believers here on earth.

Remember:

Excitement and thankfulness is a state of mind. Living a life of enjoyment is profoundly powerful and life-changing, so find time, reasons, and situations to just get excited about.

* On a scale from 1 to 10 — with 1 being your lowest and 10 being your highest: what is your level of excitement in your relationships, your health, your career, your happiness, your spirituality, and etc...? Circle your answer.

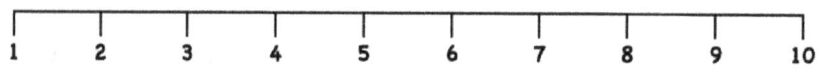

Note: Your level of excitement needs to be at a 10 in every area of your life because settling for less is not an option.

Reflective Notes

Super Excited

A MANDATORY PROTECTION

Study 3

"You must not just wear your cross, but bear your cross in this life."
~Honoré Nicole

"If any of you wants to be my [Jesus'] follower, you must turn from your selfish ways, take up your cross, and follow me."
Mark 8:34

His Priority

"He guards the path of the just..." (Proverbs 2:8 NLT)

Have you ever felt like you were in danger or felt as if something is too dangerous? Our natural tendencies signal us to run - go, leave, or try to avoid the challenging situation all together. Mentally, these dark life experiences usually cause us struggles, pressures, and trauma. These specific stress factors negatively pollute our thoughts and memories causing us to be physically and emotionally exhausted. In retrospect, these imbalanced emotions are meant to destroy us. Some examples are fear, irritability, trouble sleeping, and poor concentration. In the face of devastation, tell these evil spirits, "devil you are a liar and I rebuke you!" Refuse to allow fear and darkest to have a place in your life! We have God's promise of protection covering and balancing our path, because we are a part of the just kingdom of God.

As just people, we are obedient to the voice of God. We search for His godly wisdom, insight, and understanding to help us navigate through life's difficulties. In tough times, without reason or explanation, God makes guarding the just path His priority! So when we are stuck in these dangerous seasons, remember the Lord is Just and He will guard the path of the just. He will provide us with new perspectives. He will refresh and restore our thoughts and memories causing His justice to spring out of us, for His glory.

Choose today to disconnect from the dangers of life by relaxing on the path designated for the just. If you want the just presence of the Holy Spirit to lead your life, then say out loud: *"Lord, I praise and honor You because Your standards are True and Just, all the time! God, I love that You know everything about me, and You still take pleasure in guarding my past, present, and future path because You consider me just. Thank you for taking priority in renewing my thoughts and memories back to their original design that proves Your purpose, destiny, and perfect will for my life."*

A More In-depth Application On The Path Of The Just

* The precepts of a just person were established fully and completely in the heavenly kingdom before the creation of the earth through God the Father, Son, and Holy Spirit.

* Justly wisdom is the foundation of who God is. Due to His holy and just characteristics, we are anointed and qualified to inherit and exhibit His justly attributes here on earth.

* A just person invites God's wisdom to help them to respond righteously in stressful situations because they are in an intimate relationship (spend time) with a just God.

* A just person understands that God's wisdom goes beyond human intuition and intelligence. God is not a logical being. God is moving and working to help humanity discover and develop one's God given purpose, plan, and future.

* Just individuals long to operate in/from a spirit of excellence in one's personal and professional life. Hint, Hint: Operating in a spirit of excellence does not mean doing things perfectly or correctly all the time (no one is perfect but the Lord). Yet, it does mean giving God your very best in every area of your life and He will perfect your path.

* Just people are aware that the Word of God energizes and provides hope in both good times and challenging times.

Some Proven Characteristics That Describes A Just Person:

- A just person recognizes that Jesus actually paid the price for one to inherited His immeasurable justness.
- A just person puts confidence and trust in God
- Righteous (because Jesus is righteous)
- Holy and True
- Reasonable
- Accepts Responsibility
- Thoughtful Of Self And Others
- Have Godly Standards (standards that represent who God is)
- Yearns For The Holy Promises Of God.
- Is Motivated By Positive Change
- Accept And Recognized God's protection
- A Just Person Has A Mind That Think For Oneself.
- A Just Person Has Peace And Patience.
- A Just Person Respects And Fears God
- A Just Person Messes up! We Are Merely Humans!

Okay, let's make this real and practical. Take some time to process and cleanse your thoughts and memories from the horrible danger and fear all around you. Be still. Don't panic! Go to God in prayer and expect Him to wipe away your mental and physical horrors. The Lord takes delight in protecting the path of the just.

Right now I strongly encourage you to get serious about investing in your God-given protection. Think outside the box by looking into every area and eliminate everything in your life keeping you bogged down. Do not be afraid to confront any demonic spirit. Learn to ask God for help and be patient and be persistent, because God's protection is essential and everlasting.

Choose To Make God A Priority...

Reflective Thoughts

His Priority

 A MANDATORY PROTECTION

Study 4

"If you are going to achieve excellence in big things, you develop the habit in little matters. Excellence is not an exception, it is a prevailing attitude."
~Colin Powel

Your Want to Matters

".... and [God] protects those who are faithful to Him." (Proverbs 2:8 NLT)

Every so often, one of the greatest mental challenges we are faced with, basically deals and addresses our will. Our will reveals our heart motives, agendas, actions, and thoughts. The will and capacity of wanting to or not wanting to do something can be extremely complicated. There will be times when we want to be faithful, then other times when we do not want to be faithful. We battle with these different emotions and feelings because we are broken people in a broken world.

Momentarily, our *want to* wavers and can be easily shaken by foggy viewpoints, prejudices, layers of fears, or the misinterpretation of oneself and others. However, Jesus' **want to** is a solid and consistent foundation. The life of a believer is built

on Jesus Christ's foundation of hope and faith in this broken world. The hope and faith of Christ was first established in the heavenly realm.

God is faithful. He is loyal and reliable. His faithfulness keeps our *will* connected and dependent on His *will*. It is essential for us to develop and maintain a spiritual *want to* for His faithfulness. His faithfulness was extended to us from heaven and keeps us in direct relationship with the King of kings and the Lord of lords. The truth of the Word promised that God will protect those who are faithful to Him.

Now, let's pose this question: If God looked down from heaven would you be empowered with His divine strength and protection because your heart is faithful and you *want to* do the Lord will?

If you want to build, develop, or exercise on a deeper faith level, then say out loud. *"Lord, I am thankful Your faithfulness is perfect. Help me, Heavenly Father, to be faithful to Your overall destiny for my life in this broken world."*

A More In-depth Application On Faithfulness

* The root word for faithfulness is faith. Faith is trusting in the impossible glories of God. Faith is our foundation. Our designer and builders who builds on our foundation is God (Hebrews 11:1 10).
* Faith is not an illusion, it is a reality. Faith can transform the trajectory of your reality.
* Faith in Christ can positively affect your overall perspectives. Faith places Christ at the center of everything in your life, so your concentration in life is no longer about you and what you can achieve, but it is on how you can learn to first love, serve, and value God. Then you will learn how to display this same love, care, and value to others.
* Precisely, believers need to practice exercising faith in their daily lives. It is important that believers direct their faith to the right Source by listening, reading, and focusing on the inspired Word of God.
* Optimistically, day after day, your faith can positively increase your attitude to *want to* please the Most High. Without faith it is impossible to please God (Hebrews 11:6).
* Everyone is different, but everyone needs to walk by faith. True faith believes that God created the universe out of nothing but His spoken Word (Genesis 1).
* Everyone who is faithful will obtain His wonderful gift of protection. In order to receive this, you have to believe in the priceless blood of Christ Jesus.

* Faith gives us power to endure in times of trouble, irritability, and cultural change. Through faith, we have the supernatural power to be made strong in times of weakness.

* Take a few minutes to read about the ancient heroes' faith that still speaks in today's society (read Hebrews 11). When you read, you will find remarkable storylines of biblical faith.

Now, reflect and write down specific areas in which you know you need to work on being more faithful in. Set goals and take action to improve in these areas. Please do not be embarrassed to ask for help or work with someone who can help point you in the right direction.

Write your response here:
_____
_____
_____
_____
_____
_____

Jesus the Christ explained to His disciples "Whoever is faithful in the very little is also faithful in much…" (Luke 16:10). Regardless of life's controversies, learn to be faithful in every arena of your life because your faithfulness has an eternal reward attached to it.

Reflective Notes

Your Want to Matters

A MANDATORY PROTECTION

Study 5

"By faith, the truth of God's word is our complete Armor and Shield."
~Honoré Nicole

The Highest Level

"You are being protected by God's power through faith..." (1 Peter 1:5 HCSB)

The greatest protection you will ever need in life is already yours. In fact, the Lord's shielding is generational. God's protection chose you, your family, your children, their children, their children, and their children (Numbers 6). A divine order of safety, appointed from heaven, was commanded to flow upon you and yours. The Lord's protection was accepted and approved as manifestation in your right now life, here on earth!

In reality, the devil will try to deter you from obtaining your dimensional high level protection in these three ways. (1) Lust of the eye (desiring everything, never satisfied or content). (2) Lust of the flesh (impure craving). (3) Pride of life (he will try to persuade you to misuse power, position, prestige (read 1

John 2:15-17). With emphasis: **DO NOT** relinquish your right to access the most essential protection you will ever need or receive on this side of earth. God's protection outwits Satan's plans completely. The Spirit of God will empower and enable you with the wisdom to wrestle against any demonic spirits or temptations that come against you. With this in mind, remember, you are anointed for any wrestle, warrior!

The Lord's divine wisdom will provide you with wrestling skills to discern the Word of God over the Devil's temptations (money, fame, and/or greed). The Lord will give you holy craving that yearns after His righteousness over Satan's fleshly-lustful indulgences (sex, food, and/or any other spirit of promiscuity that leads you away from God). God has already anointed you with supernatural influence over what the world recognizes as highly influential.

If you believe the greatest protection you will ever need is already yours, then say out loud, *"Lord, by Your abundant grace through my faith in Jesus grants me access to Your high level protection. Your protection is appointed, approved, accepted, and anointed for ME. It is mine rightfully, and guess what? I WANT IT! Lord, I want Your high level protection in every area of my life."* Amen, amen, amen!

A More In-depth Application On High Level Protection

* If you want to reach a state of enjoying a life filled with God's maximum protection, then it is crucial for you to be intentional about building a committed relationship with God. Embracing this rich relationship will require you to make some sacrifices. Sacrifice your time, effort, and faithfulness.

* One of the greatest ways believers can mature spiritually is by constantly reminding themselves it is God's responsibility to provide us with heavenly protection. God specializes in dimensional protection. In fact, His protection lasts a lifetime, and is also generational.

* His protection never runs out. His protection is a free gift, but more importantly, followers of Christ must believe God's protection is for them. With knowing that His protection is for you, you also have to be responsible with your high dimensional protection as well.

Being responsible with your God-given protection means believing and obeying that everything the Word of God says is truth. We are also responsible for trusting, listening, and being sensitive to the voice of Holy Spirit that dwells within us. Being responsible requires believers to have childlike faith, a faith that resembles innocence, trust, and belief. A childlike faith believes the Word of God, no matter what!

Believe God For:

- Your Bright Future
- Strength And Wisdom
- Life
- Your Entertainment
- Family
- Your Problems
- Schooling and Education
- Neighbors and Neighborhoods
- Destiny
- Your Toxic Past
- Investment Partners
- Blessings
- The Nation's Healing
- Physical And Spiritual Protection
- Health and Freedom
- Revelation and Growth
- For Opportunities To Impact Self And Others

Believers are responsible for their own spiritual development. You must grow in your personal belief about obtaining God's dimensional protection. Having the right attitude towards His Word and teachings will stimulate growth in all areas of life.

Let's make believing God's Word correctly your life. Effective believing says, "you believe generational curses, temptations, sins, and fears were completely destroyed over two thousand years ago on the cross of Calvary. The shed blood of Jesus delivered God's children from their past, present, and future sins, fears, and the grave. Keep in mind, this does not give you a license to sin, but God wants to transform and renew your thinking so you can be used to wrestle against any evil spirit that tries to deceive and mislead you. God wants to utilize His children to expand the kingdom of God for His glory.

Let's Do A Proactive Brainstorming Exercise

Before getting started, remember, examining and identifying your distractions are necessary for spiritual and personal growth.

If you're not experiencing the abundant presence of God's protection, power, and authority within your life, I dare you to take some time and create a list of people, activities, and mindsets that may be distracting you. For instance, your list should highlight what you have been focusing on, longing for, or exalting higher than God. Then make a practical plan of action to improve in these specific areas. Regroup by shifting your focus upwards, on God's high level protection, which is already yours.

Remember: Change happens one day at a time.

Reflective Notes

The Highest Level

A MANDATORY PROTECTION

STUDY 6

"Christ is the needed hope and protection that shines in every situation"
~Honoré Nicole

"But seek first the Kingdom of God and His righteousness, and all things will be provided for you."
Matthew 6:33

Defining Moment

"For the Lamb who is at the center of the throne will shepherd them; He will guide them to springs of living waters, and God will wipe away every tear from their eyes." (Revelation 7:17 HCSB)

This is a defining moment! The Lion of Judea is on the throne! His precious presence (the spirit of God) perfects our imperfections. His shed blood cleans us, delivers us, and set us free from dark wounds, secrets, or addictions. Some of these painful experiences you may have inflicted on others or were injured by others, either way, they are harmful and hurtful. Going through these dark broken moments is tough and complex, these moments are not easy, but remember Christ is at the center of the throne. Consciously, you have to reprogram your mind and heart to grasp the truth

of knowing the blood of Jesus is on our side. His shed blood represents your redemption and your restoration on the Cross.

The blood of Jesus rescues you, fills you, reveals to you, forgives you, and releases you to receive Christ's healing power in every aspect of your life. His undeniable Word promises that God will free your soul from any fault, shame, or compulsive desires.

His shed blood promises to direct His children straight to His throne, which bears witness to His authority, power, and deity. His shed blood vowed to lead you to springs of living waters, so you would not thirst again. His shed blood promises to meet all of your daily needs. Jesus' shed blood is *perfect*, and His abundant grace and goodness vow to wipe your tears away.

Allow the defining blood of Jesus to reshape and renew your heart, mind, and soul. Look to the throne for your healing by saying out loud. *"Lord, the price Christ paid at Calvary afforded to me the greatest privilege and opportunity to receive Your unbounded grace and mercy that meets all my daily needs (spiritual, emotional, and physical). Your precious Spirit perfects my imperfections, so I am forever grateful for Christ's everlasting blood."*

A More In-depth Application On The Throne

* God's mighty power and authority is the foundation of His throne. His throne is established through righteousness (Proverbs 16:12). God is the supreme King and Ruler over His own throne.
* Fundamental elements believers receive from the throne of God are grace, mercy, glory, everlasting protection, etc.
* Biblical Scriptures emphasize that children of God have the right to come boldly to the throne of grace. Above all believers you have access to God's throne no matter what.

All your needs in life can be found at the magnificent altar of God. Do you need discipline, wisdom, self-control, hope, and/or love? If so, get serious and work hard to commit your fleshly-will to the Lord's holy will. Start by praying. Prayer is your anchor. Prayer can break through any natural flesh and will. While you praying, Jesus is at the center of the throne interceding, working, and fixing your situation in the spiritual natural realm. However, it is your responsibility take heed and receive what God is doing in your heart, mind, and soul. Be open to receive from God.

Pray About EVERTHING!

- Your attitude, perspective, and imagination
- Provision
- Job
- Finance
- Your fears and your peace
- Your hair and nails
- Areas you need to surrender to the Lord
- Supernatural wisdom and knowledge
- Your purpose, talents, gifts, and your anointing
- Family and children
- Pray for the evidence of God's signs, wonders, and miracles in your life
- Pray about what's consuming you (either healthy or unhealthy)
- Friends and your friendienemies
- Pray for the elected president and the higher governmental authorities
- Pray for the incarcerated men, women, and those individuals who are awhile trial.
- Pray over every part of your body: your mind, eyes, legs, kidneys, blood flow, and your feet, etc.
- Mental illness and trauma
- Freedom to live and feel again
- Childhood abandonment and neglect
- Your emotional state

Form A Heart of Prayer!

Through prayer the Holy Spirit will help you uncover your fleshly will and replace your will for the Lord's Will.

Okay lets be intentional: Throughout the day, take at lease 2 or 3 minutes to go to the throne of God in prayer. Allow your prayers to penetrate your heart and spirit. Believe that your prayers are moving far beyond your natural self and digging deep roots in your spirit. Believe your spirit is stronger than ever changing your attitude, mood, and mindset.

Remember: Everything that comes from the throne of God is essential for everyday living. The revelation of God's throne will be revealed His glory and protection.

Final thought: Through prayer, the power and majesty of God's throne will shine, and become surreal in the lives of believers.

Reflective Notes

Defining Moment

Study 7

"Life isn't about waiting for the storm to pass, it's about learning to dance in the [stormy] rain."
~Vivian Greene

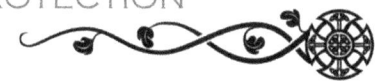

Tested and Tried

"Our lives are in his hands, and he keeps our feet from stumbling." (Psalm 66:9 NLT)

Have you ever felt as if you were being tested or tried? Tested by an arrogant boss? Tried or ridiculed for having and supporting your own political views? Tried in a legal matter by twelve jurors who were inattentive, biased, and/or in a hurry to get back to their normal lives? Tested by a failing marriage or unruly children? Tried and ostracized by religious people? Tried and tested by unexpected grief (the loss of someone or something)?

Usually, in the midst of all of these circumstances we are left feeling confused, empty, and helpless. However, the psalmist reminded believers to stay strong in their difficulties, because the Lord will not allow our feet to slip or stumble. **Read Psalm 66:9 AMP.**

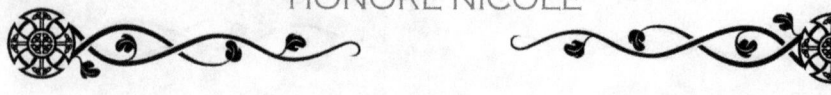

It is important that you know God sees and cares for you! He has a specific plan and purpose to fulfill in this world and in your life. **Read Jeremiah 29:11.**

In the middle of any situation, we have the assurance we are safe in the palms of the Master's hands. We believe the Creator has the authority to control ALL things. He allow us to safely surrender our will for His. If you share this belief, then say out loud: *"Lord, I trust and believe You with all my heart. I am certain that these stumbling blocks will not defeat me. I praise You, Yahweh, because You know what's best for me."*

A More In-depth Application On Our Lives Being In The Master's Hands

* The Sovereign hands of God represent divine protection, blessings, direction, power, provision, correction, and guidance.
* An image of the Lord's hands is also a beautiful expression of His unconditional love (it is not based on our behaviors or conditions, but solely because of His perfect nature and character).
* The Lord's hands are distinctively different from human hands. Human hands are tangible (made of flesh, they can be seen and touched). The awesome hands of the all Powerful are theoretical (spiritual, they are invisible). God's infinite hands are what distinguish His hands from the finite hands of humans.
* The hands of the Lord are gracious and merciful in the of best of times and even in the worst of times.
* God sees, shares, cares, and even allows hardships. However, the Lord's incomparable hands keep the righteous secure. You can trust yourself in the Lord's hands because He promised never to fail you — He is committed to you.
* The hands of the Lord are persistent. He will protect you from any danger, evil schemes, and foolishness.
* Do not be surprised by the fact that the Lord's hands can also keep you from advancing too soon. He knows when you

will reach your level of maturity that provokes you to advance in faithfulness.

* God's hands are sure and steady, so do your best to put your life in His hands.

* The Lord's intrinsic hands allow you to live spiritually whole, through Christ's shed blood. You have all the neccessary tools for your day, your life, your career, your ministry, your spirit and space, your passions, and even your uncertainties to live a life of victory, because everything you need has already been established in heaven for you.

Take a moment to close your eyes and envision yourself walking into the awesome hands of the Almighty. Now, lay down in the palms of those hands and rest. Imagine how it feels for His hands to encircle you. Now can you feel the constant flow of safety, comfort, and love within those hands?

Remember, God is our primary Guardian, so we can trust Him with all of our cares. So today, let's vow to become more appreciative for the protection that freely comes from the Master's hands.

Reflective Notes

Tested and Tried

Study 8

You can trust that God is...

- Creator and Ruler over the universe,
- Sovereign,
- Almighty,
- In Control,
- A Protector,
- A Healer,
- A Deliverer,
- Holy,
- Lord over all,
- Faithful and True,
- Counting on you.

THE ESSENCE OF WHO GOD IS

"God is our refuge and strength, a helper who is always found in times of trouble." (Psalm 46:1 HCSB)

If you are being honest with yourself, people across the globe, everywhere, are going through some form of trouble, tragedy, or tension, either big or small. If you are not going through anything, then that is a true blessing. However, I am sure you know someone who is struggling with something. No one is exempt from rainy days. Rain is guaranteed in life. Yet, when rain falls, your perception of who GOD IS, in these seasons matters.

The psalmist encouraged believers to put their hope and consideration on who GOD IS in times of troubles. Remember, GOD IS your 'refuge' (shelter, a place where we can find peace), GOD IS your 'strength' (might, power, His love empowers you with the strength to stand firm in any situation), and GOD IS your 'helper' (a partner— you do not have to go through life alone).

In God, believers (hint, hint: you) have an advantage of putting on water resistant rain gear (seek God for deliverance) when ominous weather is in the forecast. While it does not feel or look good, if we give God our full attention, He will give us strength to rise above the rain falls of life. The rain falls of life contribute to growth (maturity), but remain hopeful, because a rainbow usually come after the rain. Remember: A rainbow is a sign that you made it through the storm because — GOD IS.

If you believe supernatural purpose comes out of the rains of life, then say out loud. "*Lord, I realize in Christ, I place my faith, hope, and consideration. I already know You brought me through the rain, so I want to take this moment to thank the Holy Spirit for empowering me with the might to handle any weather because my hope and trust is totally dependent upon who GOD IS.*"

A More In-depth Application On The Essence Of Who GOD IS

The palmist gave a clear picture of who GOD IS in times of trouble:

* Refuge, strength, and helper are three words to describe the gracious and merciful character of who GOD IS in tough times. He is our 'refuge,' a covering that protects us. He is the shield that goes before us in times of danger and devastation. Figuratively and spiritually, God is a safe dwelling place where we can find comfort and peace.

* God is our 'strength,' a divine power that enables us to endure struggles with courage and confidence. Seeking Him first must be our priority in all we do. The Lord will provide us with the might to do His great work here on earth.

* God is our 'helper,' a supernatural partner who is Equipped and Ready to provide help in times of need. He is an invisible supporter who will fight against any evil principality that comes against His children (your vindicator). **Read Deuteronomy 32:35 Romans 12:19.**

* The psalmist used three nouns to highlight who God is. If you are being transparent with yourself, most individuals typically seek God when faced with opposition. In fact, it is during seasons of opposition that most people learn to trust put confidence in God.

* Generally and humanly, a person usually does not just automatically put his or her trust in God. Trust is not a fast process and it takes time. Trust is a safe emotion. Trust goes through

seasons of ups and downs, but always stands firm. Trust is a confidence that individuals develop within close intimate relationships (not sexual, but relationships that are near and dear to the heart), but Kingdom trust and confidence is essential in the world you live in today.

* The one true God, the creator of the universe, wants to be in a close intimate relationship with 'you'. Unbelievable right? Well, it is true. However, in order to receive all of His glorious benefits, you have to be willing to first give up your agenda (your will, your way, your ideas, and your plans) for His agenda (for His will, His way, His idea, and His plans). Exchange your agenda for His Holy agenda.

* In reality, it is essential for us to learn to SEEK AND DEPEND ON THE MOST HIGH FOR EVERYTHING, AT ALL TIMES. Seek and depend on His Spirit for the big and small things. For example, throughout the day, consciously, you have to learn to grow, by seeking to be a part of God's beautiful plan for your life. God covers you with His presence and His love — you are never alone. He promised to be your invisible helper. He takes delight in taking care of his needy children (Psalm 107:9).

* God is the creator of Everything (every good thing), and you need Him for everything, because His presenjce is real and God is powerful.

Now let's do a writing exercise. Grab a sheet of paper and something to write with. Take a few seconds to quiet down your mind, thoughts, and spirit from any distractions. Write down specific areas where you know you need to consciously seek

and depend on the Spirit more. Areas where you acknowledge you need more shelter, more strength, and more of His help in.

If you know God is God, not just in troublesome situations, but in all situations. Then pray out loud, *"Lord, I am sorry for doubting You in times of troubles and depending on you only when it is convenient for me. I invite you into every detail and moment of my life. I am aware that you know everything about me and am in awe because You still desire to draw near to me today, tomorrow, and forevermore."*

Reflective Notes

The Essence of Who God Is

A MANDATORY PROTECTION

Study 9

"Living a life of constant praise and worship has the supernatural power to transform your life. You can move from living your worst life, to you living a good life, to you living your best life."
~Honoré Nicole

Increase Your Praise

"Look, I have given you the authority to trample on snakes and scorpions and over all the power of the enemy nothing will ever harm you." (Luke 10:19 HCSB)

Ultimately, the body of Christ is on a mission and the mission purpose: Is for the church of the Lord to offer up and exalt continual praise *for* the divine character *of* God, as top priority. Praise is one of the greatest admirations God takes delight in. For instance, the Messiah knew He was on a sacred earthly mission assignment for Abba— His Heavenly Father. For this reason, Christ's vocation in life was to teach the body of Christ to discover how to keep their body and soul together in harmony by living a life of constant praise and worship until their individual mission on earth is FINISHED. Jesus displayed holy honor and worship in times of love, intentional pain, humiliation, death, and His resurrection.

Universally, God created everything in creation to praise Him, including humanity (Psalm 103:22). All of God's children have a real reason to increase their praise. Your praise must rise up especially in turbulent times of: Crime violence, character assassination, racial discrimination, culture instability, unemployment, fighting against one's own demons, police brutality, financial crises, fear, mass incarceration, and all other noisy machines that you are subjected to *day in* and *day out*.

However, Jesus' words are still fundamentally speaking *in* and *to* today's modern day culture. As an imperfect person, Christ invested within you power, authority, and protection to trample **on** and **over** snakes (danger) and scorpions (evil and unclean spirits emotionally, physically, and figuratively). In fact, this is a perfect time for you to turn away from the fake ways and superficial things the world expects you to praise by increasing your Kingdom praise. Kingdom praise is an active eruption of pure praise that takes place immediately in the hearts anjd minds of all God's children.

Keep in mind, praise is NOT restricted to music, singing, musical instruments, or dancing. Praise is an expression of speaking, declaring, living, and proclaiming a rhythm of intimate peace, joy, power, love, and authority that only comes through the greater grace and mercy of Jesus Christ. With this in mind, don't bury your praise, increase your praise, let your praise be heard, let your praise go ahead of you and create new opportunities and blessings for your destiny.

Basically, your praise is your hope forward or your way out of any situation. Allow your praise to grow and shape your journey in life by saying out loud: *"Lord, I realize the aroma of my praise pleases You. So, I don't want to miss the opportunity to elevate true praise. Praise is one of the greatest gifts You entrusted to me, so by faith, I humbly offer up all my praise to You, my Lord and Savior, Jesus Christ."*

A More In-depth Application of Increasing Your Praise

* Praise is an *art* and *act* of directly worshipping the Life and Lordship of Jesus Christ, as God Almighty.
* A life of real praise reflects the authenticity of everything you say and do.
* Praise unlocks God's supernatural peace and rest to flow in your life.
* The power of praise is an overall heavenly form of communication in which you use to convey a message of awe and agreement that Jesus Christ is worthy of all honor and worship.
* Praise is sacred, and it matters to God!
* Praise is an energizing melody that lives in the hearts of all God's children. (Ephesians 5:19). By faith, praise affirms real joy, strength, and hope. **Study Nehemiah 8:10**.
* Abundant praise is a heartwarming solid substance that is already generating in the DNA of all God's children.
* Praise inspires an even greater reason for believers to glorify, honor, and worship the gracious nature and character of God. Praise also stimulates spiritual growth and motivates believers to love one's neighbor as oneself. **Study Matthew 22:37-39.**
* Holistically, followers of Christ are fortunate because the Holy Spirit has empowered His children with perfect praise (power) and authority to increases one's praise under all forms of evil and destruction connected to the kingdom of darkness. **Study Luke 10:18-19.**

A MANDATORY PROTECTION

* Praise produces an overflow of thankfulness and respectfulness to and for the reflective nature of who God is. It is a deep affection believers show through their actions and attitudes.

* Through Jesus Christ, universal praise is available. God desires for all of humanity to experience true worship. The essence of God is worthy and deserving of ALL glory, ALL honor, and ALL praise.

Why Is Praise Crucial?

- Praise acknowledges that God is sovereign over ALL things.
- The wisdom and knowledge of your praise will bring your speech, thoughts, career, passions, compassions, writings, arts, and self-esteem to a higher new level.
- Personal praise is a personal devotion, which help you learn and develop to be the person God created you to already BE.
- A heart of praise destroys yokes, and breaks through strongholds and bondages.
- Abundant praise is an true investment that fights against evil and wicked spirits making God's children effective.
- Praise is therapeutic in highly stressful times.
- Praise is a privilege and a blessing that builds stability in uncertain times.
- True praise intimidates the author of confusion (Satan).
- Praise disrupts any public or personal disfunctions.
- Declaration of praise ignites power, strength, deliverance, protection, healing, and victory.
- Expression of praise encourages servants of God to bring all of one's wants, desires, and needs to the throne of the Almighty King at all times.

- Praise does not just affect the individual person: authentic praise changes communities and generations.
- Praise is necessary and it keeps the Holy Spirit active in every arena of one's life.
- Praise on the level you desire God to take you too.
- Praise creates new opportunities, clearer visions, and provides the person with a clear sense of one's self.
- Praise is the access that leads believers to walk in the invading, impossible, intangible, mighty favors and anointing of God.
- Maximum praise equips God's children to fight against negativity.
- Praise provides the basis for the radiance of God's presence to shine bright in all situations.
- Praise strengthens believers courageously. Praise is a spiritual devotion and discipline that releases believers from any festering or unaddressed hurt or pain. Believers must allow their praise to be centered on God the Father, Son, and Holy Spirit at all times.

Pause and Ponder:

What would this world look like if the body of Christ lived a life of praise, rather than living a life of problems?
Allow your praise on earth to reach far above all the heavens in refill the earth with joy.

Remember:

The Lord is worthy of all praise because He is in control, and His divine purpose will be fulfilled in His Kingdom as it is established on earth.

Reflective Notes

Increase Your Praise

REFLECTIVE NOTES

INCREASE YOUR PRAISE

Study 10

"You must dismantle your idols, or your idols will dismantle you."
~Honoré Nicole

Dismantle Your Idols

"Little children, guard yourselves from idols." (1 John 5:21 HCSB)

In this already anxious world, several ideas, situations, and people are fighting for your attention daily. If you are not careful, you will look to: individuals, accomplishments, material possessions, professional careers, and wealth for: safety, comfort, and fulfillment. Gradually, without notice, the above things will consume you and you will start exalting them higher than God.

For instance, in today's culture, there are many modern day idols you can give life to. Simply put, idols are fake gods that seem real. They provide false hope that people put assurance and confidence in. For example, have you ever given all of yourself to your children, their activities, or their education and not given God any of your focus? Have you ever tried to

work endlessly for approval or acceptance of others? Are you egocentric, and God has no room in your equation (your life)? Have you ever cherished a fruitless relationship by assuming you had the power to make it fruitful? Do you look to social media for validations or to find your identity by dedicating all of your time and attention to receiving media 'likes'? Do you need to be in control or have control over every situation, and if you don't, do you feel like a failure? Do you take credit for your success or financial gain, instead of thanking God for His generous provisions?

Ouch! Did any of those illustrations hit home for you? If you answered *yes* to any of the above questions, it is okay. In retrospect, you were entrusted with all of these gifts from God to enjoy, but the issue comes in when you allow these same blessings to take precedence over God being first priority in your life. It is imperative that you understand that everyone is guilty of worshipping idols at some point or another, we are merely human. Yet, the protection of God's grace give you (His child) a corrective power and opportunity to dismantle faulty idols. Daily, you must be intentional about tearing down anything that is stopping God from being first priority in your life. If not, externally, you may believe you are flourishing, but spiritually you are doomed, because God is the ultimate gift Giver, so you must put Him back in the center your life.

Let's destroy the idols you may have created for yourself by saying out loud: *"Lord, I thank you for blessing me with all of your gifts and provisions. Teach me Holy Spirit how to give them all back to You. I am sorry for foolishly insulting You by highly exalting physical blessings over You. I want You to help me, with the faith of Christ, to remove and replace everything in my heart, mind, and soul that is leading me away from You. Guide me Spirit, show me how to elevate you Lord, higher than my idols."*

A More In-depth Application On Dismantling Your Idols

* Idols are people, places, and things people usually subconsciously worship and praise, taking their attention off of the Lord. Idols are connected to idolatry.
* Idolatry is a deceiving spirit. Please read carefully, EVERYTHING IN OUR LIVES IS CONNECTED TO A SPIRIT. EITHER A GODLY SPIRIT OR AN EVIL SPIRIT.
* Idols are fake gods. They appear to be pure, but they are really impure.
* The Lord, the Creator of both heaven and earth, is a jealous God. **Read Exodus 20:5.** He REFUSES to share His honor and glory with worthless false gods. The Word of God warns humanity not to *put* or *find* security in fake gods. If so, traveling down the road of idolatry will be terrifying and lonely.
* Idols can keep us spiritually blinded from the presence of God Almighty. If we take pleasure in worshiping idols, over God's presence, then we are in spiritual darkness. For "no man can serve two masters. For you will hate one and love the other." (Matthew 6:24).
* The fundamental presence of God indicates that "God is with us." See Matthew 1:23.

Let's Unmask Some Modern Day Idols That We Often Surrender Our Spiritual Power To...

- Social Media
- Careers or Profits
- Pain From The Past
- Cultural Fame
- Pride
- Custom Cars
- All Forms of Abuse
- Achievements
- The Love of Money
- Others' Opinions
- Recognition and Attention
- Trauma
- Fear
- Your Heart
- Designer Clothes
- Video games, ect.

All of these things can rob you of your joy, but the blood of Jesus can restore that joy and peace back to you. Let's develop putting and keeping God at the core of your life, and everything else will be added to you (Matthew 6:33).

Your relationship with God is foundational. Therefore, let's learn to explore some ways you can ensure the Lord is essential in every area of your life. Below are five simple principles on how to involve the Lord in your daily life:

(1) When your eyelids open in the morning, before your feet ever hit the floor, tell the Lord good morning. Thank Him for allowing you to see another day, and glorify Him by acknowledging and recognizing His awesomeness in your life.
(2) Invite the Holy Spirit into every area of your life. Did you know the Spirit has a deep yearning to be a part of your family, your quiet time, your finances, your decision making, your social groups, your mental state, and your personal and professional plans?
(3) Spend quality time reading, studying, and applying the Lord's instructions to your daily life.
(4) Remember what Jesus said, "Wherever your treasure is, there your heart will be also" (Matthew 6:21). Throughout the day intentionally ponder on the goodness of who God is in your life.
(5) At the end of the day, take a few minutes to thank God for protecting and keeping you and your loved ones safe. Ask Him to continue to watch over the nation and remind Him that you want to rest peacefully in His presence all night.

Pray this prayer silently to yourself: *"Lord, above all else, I know how much I need you. I trust You for my safety, comfort, and fulfilment. No other gods can amount to who You are in my life. Above all, by the power of the Holy Spirit, I need you to actively help me to physically pull down and remove anything that pressures me from rightly exalting you. I am a part of your royal priesthood, and I am chosen to worship You — Lord above all else. I ask these things in Christ Jesus' name, Amen."*

Remember:

Idols cannot protect you. Idols are worthless and useless, so dismantle your idols and go back to your first love. **Read Isaiah 30:22.**

Reflective Notes

Dismantle Your Idols

REFLECTIVE NOTES

A MANDATORY PROTECTION

STUDY 11

"A greatest treasure are those invisible to the eye, but found by the heart." ~Judy Garland.

The Greatest Treasure

"He grants a treasure of common sense to the honest. He is shield to those who walk with integrity." (Proverbs 2:7 NLT)

An honest person, one who walks in integrity, will be covered by the presence of the Almighty. One will maintain divine wisdom, knowledge, and understanding from God, one's Heavenly Father. However, you have to be willing to be a student (hungry and thirst after righteousness) who desires to listen, look, and learn from the Lord's teachings and guidance. Would you like to be a student in the Most High classroom? If so, the power of the Word provide believers with supernatural promises of everlasting mercy, peace, and blessings.

Remember, in real life situations, disappointments will occur, but refrain from compromising or devaluing your val-

ue system. Instead be open to allowing His righteousness to flourish in your heart, mind, and spirit. The abundant grace of the blood shed by Jesus is already filled with all the honesty and integrity you would ever need, yet it is your responsibility keep and maintain His honesty and integrity.

If you are intentionally striving to be honest, and a person of integrity, then say out loud: *"Lord, I diligently seek your wisdom by securing your truth in my innermost being. I believe my life is anointed and blessed by the power of your Divine Holy Spirit, because God himself is my greatest treasure imaginable."*

A More In-depth Application Of Walking In Honesty and Integrity

* Both words honesty and integrity are communicable attributes (qualities that God handed down to humanity) of God.
* God is honest. Integrity is a part of His divine nature.
* Genesis 1:27-28 demonstrates how humanity was created in the same image of God the Father, Son, and Holy Spirit (The Trinity - Christian Doctrine - Three-in-one God).
* The image of God is not a physical form, but a supernatural spiritual form.
* As a child of God you have the right to attain honesty and integrity in every area of your life, because you mirror the righteous standards of our Creator.
* The Kingdom of Heaven is where righteous standards begin and end. God's dwelling place is valuable. His domain is like treasure hidden in a field. (Matthew 13:44-45)

Attributes Of An Honest Person Who Walks With Integrity:

- Isn't A Perfect Person
- Trustworthy
- Loving
- Completely Dependent On God
- Whole, Healthy, and Balanced In Different Stages of Life
- Practice Holiness And Righteousness
- Speak truth From The Heart In Love

- Has Unmovable Faith
- Has A Good Reputation
- Keeps One's Words And Actions From Various Forms Of Evil.
- Diligent
- A Peacemaker, etc.

The imagery of God being a shield for anyone who follows the advice and instructions of His words will inherit all of His magnificent qualities that He entrusted to His followers.

Make every effort to ensure your words and actions act in accordance to what is upright and pure by listening, looking, and learning to seek the Lord's communicable qualities.

Let's meditate on Matthew 5:6, " Blessed are those who hunger and thirst for righteousness, for they shall obtain mercy."

God Himself is your greatest treasure.

Reflective Notes

The Greatest Treasure

A MANDATORY PROTECTION

Study 12

"So when God looks at you now, He no longer sees your humanity, your frailty, your sin... your unrighteousness. He sees you through the blood-stained filter of his own Son, the perfect Lamb of God. You no longer need to exhaust yourself striving for perfection. You are alreaedy completely, wholly, and perfectly righteous because of Christ's gift to you."
~Priscilla Shirer

Most Qualified Defender

"In every situation take the shield of faith, and with it you will be able to extinguish all the flaming arrows of the evil one." (Ephesians 6:16 HCSB)

In the face of fear, a global pandemic, criticism, injustice prevalent in today's culture, single parenthood, rejection, incarceration, inflation, serious illness, and so forth (because this list goes on), the Apostle Paul's words commanded believers to lift up the shield of faith. The Lord hears our distinctive concerns and cries, and He has already answered our calls for help. Because He is infallible (It is impossible for Him to make a mistake) and has supernatural characteristics, we can trust that He will meet every one of your needs.

In the middle of distress, it is our responsibility to lift up the shield of faith by confirming your trust in the Lord. Recognize and acknowledge that all of the devil's evil attacks are rendered powerless under the shield of faith. Keep in mind: You are in a trusted relationship with God, your ultimate Protector.

As an expression of gratitude for Christ's continuous shield and seal of protection in your life, say out loud: "*Lord, regardless of the treacherous dangers that I have and will face in this life, I am not afraid, because you are the Most Qualified Defender and my trust and faith is in You.*"

A More In-depth Study On The Shield of Faith

* The shield of faith is literally trusting in God "No Matter What."
* Trusting in God while in tremendous (GOOD) times.
* Trusting in God while in treacherous (BAD) times.
* Trusting can be as simple as putting faith in someone who is reliable (God).
* Putting your trust in Christ requires action (James 2:20). Your actions can be prayer, reading, meditating on the Word of God, and applying the wisdom and knowledge of God to specific situations in your life.
* When you put trust in the Messiah, you are actually verbalizing (sometimes without words). He will deal with your particular matter.

Trust Is:

- A Reflection Of God's Glory
- Putting Confidence In
- Focusing On God's Truth
- Placing Hope In
- Imaging Or Reimaging God's Goodness And Faithfulness.
- Relying On
- Having Peace In The Most Difficult Circumstances.
- Trusting in God's Supernatural Assurance!!!

Trusting in God can be a gradual and delicate process. However, when you tap into the supernatural abundance, power, and care of the Holy Spirit within you, you will recognize (why) it is essential for you to lift up the shield of faith. You will then be given the grace to learn and grow in both spirit and practicality.

I urge you to write down and pray Ephesians 3: 20-21 over your life and circumstances, because trusting in the plan of God can give you exceedingly more than what you could ever ask, think, or imagine.

Pray these Scriptures with me: *"Now to Him who is able to do above and beyond all that we ask or think according to the power that works in us to Him be glory in the church and in Christ Jesus to all generations, forever and ever. Amen."* **Read Ephesians 3:20-21.**

A MANDATORY PROTECTION

Reflective Notes

Most Qualified Defender

Just Think

How are you trusting God to orchestrate His protection in your life, your loved one's life, and in the world encircling you? Write down 12 different ways you are depending on receiving God's protection in your life like never before. This may seem strange—but please take your time in Think:

1. _____
2. _____
3. _____
4. _____
5. _____
6. _____
7. _____
8. _____
9. _____
10. _____
11. _____
12. _____

_____   _____

Signature   Date

Signing means you are confirming and expressing that you are open to intentionally search, seek, and depend on God's invisable presence and protection in every area of life. If you stay in forward motion, you will be amazed at how God's protection is inclusive and exclusively for you!

JUST THINK

Jobs are the primary job information. His orders is to wonder particular difficult in light in the world are like. At times, at times you are dependent to ecotourists are good many for life necessitates in town, or more i'm sure take you up from

Symptoms	Date

Stating means you are comfortable and expressing. The simple statement bar, sounds, were, and thoughtful a task versatile praises, and experience every thought life. If you start to award yourself, you will not ensure of how. Stop play rather a mellow and hold you in thought.

Congratulations, you finished! Please cut out and frame.

Acknowledgements of Praise

I am reminded through the Word of God that in everything give thanks. Therefore, " I give thanks to Christ Jesus our Lord who has strengthened me, because He considered me faithful, appointing me to the ministry" (1 Timothy 1:12). I am extremely honored and humbled by the vast amount of people He has entrusted and blessed me with to help His vision He gave me come into fruition.

Ms. Quincy, Mr. Frank, and the entire Cadmus Publishing staff: thank you for believing and having faith in my vision. I honestly enjoyed every aspect of my publishing experience. You all are phenomenal and so amazing. The things that should have been complicated for me, you all made simple, straightforward, and possible.

To Governor John Bel Edwards, First Lady Donna H. Edward, Secretary James M. Le Blanc, Malcolm Meyers, Natalie Laborde and all governmental officials: Thank you for being extraordinary, God-fearing leaders who totally displayed on several occasions "in-person" that you all care about the minds, hearts, and needs of all the women in this facility. I was elated to be in the presence of all of you. You all created a positive environment, with positive aroma, where several women acknowledged that we felt heard, understood, but more importantly, we felt your genuine love and cared for. Thank you for being uplifting leaders who are not afraid to make challenging decisions with clear-sightedness, foresight, power, and integrity, which is positively captivating the Louisianians' needs.

To the ministries teams working behind the gates: Chief Chaplain Debi Sharkey, Dr. Kristi Miller-Anderson, Campus Pastor Mrs. Ann, Brother Mike, Pastor Mike and First Lady Rachel, and the entire Healing Place Church. Family of God brother Glynn and Mrs. Barbara, Full Gospel Mrs. Marsha and Mr Dennis, and Mrs. Barbara, Rejoice Ministry Sister Joyce, Bishop Butler and the whole St. Luke church family and to the several donors and spouse who are not mentioned. Thank you for believing in revival behind the gates. I'm grateful that God loves us and He uses all of you as His mighty instruments to spread the Good News. With that truth in mind, your consistence and faithfulness is expanding the kingdom of God. A very special thanks to the New Orleans Baptist Theological Seminary (NOBTS) for having the vision and belief that higher education through the presentation of God's Word is precedent in redeeming the lost women behind the barbed wire. Without donors, professors and adjunct faculty my vision would never have come to fruition but where God gives vision, he provides provision. Thank you for answering God's call.

Television Ministries: The Word Network, Hillsong, TBN, and sort forth: Only by the grace of the Almighty, the "Potter's House" "Enjoying Everyday Living" "Pastor Joel Osteen and First Lady Victoria Osteen" "Changing the World Network" "Elevation Church", and so many other ministries who are globally and intentionally—preaching and teaching the Word of God with grace, power, passion, enjoyment, and within a spirit of excellence. Thank you for providing inspirational programs, which challenged me to pursue God, the Father, the Son, and the Holy Spirit for teaching me how to look above for all my physical and spiritual needs. I am grateful that these television ministries broadcast worldwide, which includes the world that most of society has "marked out."

Before there was ever *A Mandatory Protection* study, there were several great men and women who wrote on the importance of God's Protection. Thank you: C.S Lewis, Priscilla Shirer, Joseph Prince, and Max Lucado, for being the daily voice millions of people don't mind listening to.

To the many beautiful ladies behind the gates: Thank you for your contributions to this study. Please know I am grateful for your countless number of hours you took out your precious day to read, edit, provide helpful feedback, and for your creative art skills for my cover. I am grateful for your diligence and abilities on helping this study become a reality. A special thanks to you Gaspard. D, Houston. M, Kitts. M, Mills. J, Mulla. L, Monaco. S, Rathore. A, Saltzman. C, Simms. S, Smith. T, Staggs. C, and Starks. T for leaving your fingerprints on helping this study becoming a bestselling Bible Study that will help many people understand that God's divine protection is especially for them. Thank you for serving and believing that I had sometime meaningful to share with the world.

B.B.U author Monique Houston: thank you for inspiring me week after week to write. Without your support, this study would just be a figment of my imagination or just chatter in a meaningless conversation. Your encouragement and support reminds me of the Nike slogan, "Just Do It." Thank you girl, from the depths of my heart for always believing in me. Smile bright, Ms. Resilient. I love you!

Surtanti, Katherine, Tonye, Ms. Monique, Ms. Darlene, Tracey, Tamika, and Carr: I am grateful for our friendship, and I am thankful for your love, support, and your presence in my life. Your wisdom, guidance, and prayers motivated me to be

the BEST me—in the good, bad, and other times. Each one of you are invaluable to me personally and mandatory pieces to my spiritual fitness journey. Love you!

To my one and only sister, Crystal: You are beautiful, incredible, and you excel in strength. Having you as my sister is one of the many highlights of my day. When the odds are stacked high against us—thank you for your greatness, your commitment, and for being my BEST friend before the creation of this world. On purpose and with purpose, sister you always, always chose me, respected me, looked up to me, and love me as your big sister. Thank you for being my cheerleader. I love you sister today, tomorrow, and forevermore.

To the amazing medical department behind the gates: thank you from the bottom of my heart for being tremendously supportive. You were key parts that help shape this study. I appreciate and value each one of you.

To my small groups: Thank you Adams. C, Bowers. E, Ervin. K, Frank. A, and Heard. A—for being great listeners. Your support inspires me to push forward. I am grateful for your presence in my life. Thank you for investing in me. I love you.

To my brothers, Derrick and Byron: I am grateful that both of you shower me with nothing but brotherly love. All you ever asked of me is for me to grow, evolve, and soar higher than both of you. Generally speaking, you all challenged me to win by reminding me to stand tall in the face of opposition, stay focused on purpose, and you all drilled in my heart, mind, and spirit that "it is in God we trust." Thank you for being my BB's (big brothers) for life.

To my late brothers Mark and Joe: You all received your invisible wings way too soon. Honestly speaking, it was extremely hard to let you guys go. So trillion times over, I love you, and trillion times over, I miss you, and trillion times over, I am grateful that you all are now in the protective presence of the Most High. Here is a message from the entire family: We are sending all our love above to your new heavenly home.

To my maternal aunts: Dianne, Margo, Shelia, and Threa: Since I was a young girl, you all summed up the definition of godly love. You cherish His love in your hearts through words, actions, and your lifestyles. Daily, you all displayed "why" I needed to be in close relationship with Christ, our Lord and Savior. You all were the critical genesis and essence that helped me learn how to tap into becoming the woman God created me to be. In hindsight, I admire the way all of you love the Lord, which left an everlasting impact on my brain and heart. Thank you for all your wisdom, expertise, prayers, and for being godly examples.

To all of my aunts, uncles, nieces, nephews, and cousins: I'm grateful that all of you always allowed me to just be me. Each one of you is a mandatory piece of the puzzle God has designed me to be. Family is everything. I love you. Thank you for enveloping me in your love.

To Mr. Uyles and Mrs. Rhoda, and the entire church family: I would like to express my gratitude for your support and for earnestly praying for me, my family, and my physical freedom. Thank for your compassion, and I love each of you.

To Mr. Sheldon and Mrs. Andrea: In my worst hours, your patience, support, love, faith and faithfulness was incredibly warranted during the most difficult time of my life. Thank you for being the chief caregivers that made sure I remained active and fully involved in every aspect of my eldest son's life. Because of your wisdom and insight, today we cherish and value our unbreakable mother/son relationship.

To my two sons: you two are the greatest blessings God could have ever entrusted to me. I love you so much and I just want to thank you for loving me and supporting me unapologetically. Both of you are my greatest pride and my greatest joy and all my motherly love is for both of you. I love you always and forever.

To my +one daughter: You are special and truly loved. Live your life with vision and courage no matter what.

To my mom and my dad, if there was no you than it would not be a me. Thank you for saying 'yes' to God by giving me my life, my purpose, and my ministry. To be honest, what God is doing in my life is bigger than you, it is bigger than me, it is bigger than us, because at the end of my story, God will get the glory! I love you momma, I love you daddy, I love you both more than you could ever know!

To my grandmother Irma: By the grace of God, because of your influence and impact, I am sure I am a daughter of the Most High. I always was and forever will Be. Grandma, you were and still are my solid rock. You cared for my physical, natural, and spiritual needs. Your fragrance of love, care, and encouragement, went alone with your spice of correction, which is still meeting my specific needs today. Irmaie, you were full of life and wisdom, and in my immaturity, I was to blinded to cherish and appreciate your due diligence in which you faithfully displayed to everyone. Your incredible life, love, beauty, nourishment, healing, and protectiveness intensify within me—greater life. Thank you for giving me the best intangible gift any person could ever obtain, JESUS! The protection of God is an invaluable and mandatory gift, so I am passing on the same wisdom you gave me to other beautiful souls on the globe. P.S. Me and you against the world!

Finally, my deepest thanks goes out to all of you. I know this study will reach the lives of those unknown to me, but I appreciate your support and thank you for believing in the mandatory protection of God, Almighty. In every way, each day, God's divine protection is perfect, challenging, intentional, safe, beautiful, and it includes E-V-E-R-Y-O-N-E.

About the Author

Honoré Nicole is a mother of two brilliant sons first, but through life experiences she has learned to acknowledge and recognize the greatest gift of God's protection extended to her through the overflowing grace of her Lord and Savior, Jesus Christ. She has earned Associate and Bachelor's Degrees in Christian Ministry with a minor in Biblical Studies. As she continues to pursue her Master's of Theology, you'll learn why she is certain that God's divine protection is all around her, all over her, within her, and goes far beyond her. As a first-time author, she desires for this Bible Study to travel across the globe and become a bestselling study. She knows God's protection is for everyone, but only a few understand it, attain it, and apply it. Her family's roots are ruminating in a nearby city outside of New Orleans, Louisiana, and she is confident that God gave her the faith and wisdom to write this study, so in her daily life, she is consciously allowing the protection of God to just BE.

Additional Contact Information

Address: Post Box 26, St. Gabriel, LA 70776
Email: Securus Mobile App or amandatoryprotection@gmail.com and you can graciously give at Paypal.
Paypal: amandatoryprotection@gmail.com

Remember: God's supernatural protection is protecting you through His divine power